Historic Bath

Written by Diana Winsor

Introduction

Bath is something of a paradox among European cities. It sits as comfortably as a sleepy cat in a curve of the River Avon, but it probably owes as much to ancient Rome as to the surrounding snug green English countryside. Its stone reflects sunshine more happily than it absorbs soft English rain. It is an Italianate confection of honey-coloured stone which has nevertheless played a unique part in the social and architectural history of Britain.

An accident of geology was responsible for the founding of Bath more than 2,000 years ago, when some early man, one of the Celts who measured time by darkness and marked their lives by the seasons, first came upon a place where snow never lay and a strange vapour hung over oozing waters. Hot springs fed them. It was a place of magic power, and so it was dedicated to the Celtic deity Sul, to whose name the Romans later linked that of their goddess Minerva. And when the Roman Empire fell, the sacred baths fed by the steaming waters were restored by men of another faith: Christianity.

The monks of the great Benedictine monastery at Bath ran the hot baths for several centuries, attracting increasing numbers of people who believed in the healing qualities of the water. By the end of the seventeenth century the city council had taken over responsibility for them, and was becoming aware of their profitable potential. New attractions were offered besides the sometimes dubious one of dressing up in yellow canvas and being immersed in often unsavoury green water. Gambling, by then a national fever, began to flourish in the city. People of fashion with money and time to spend sought summer diversion out of London, and found it in Bath. Georgian Bath was beginning.

Three men were to be indentified with this great expansion of the city, and with the spirit of the age. Ralph Allen, a man of humble origins but a brilliant entrepreneur, saw the potential in the hitherto neglected Bath stone, and commissioned a visionary young architect called John Wood to display its quality. At the same time Bath society itself was being transformed by an impoverished young gambler and dandy from Wales called Richard 'Beau' Nash, who became self-appointed king of his own idiosyncratic empire within John Wood's unparalleled setting.

Pulteney Bridge from Parade Gardens

aunts and liverish retired colonels. Not until recent years has it been restored to its original beauty, with more than a century of blackening soot cleaned from the porous grey and amber limestone. Damage done during wartime bombing and the subsequent depredations of insensitive city planners has been to a large extent restored. Bath is in fashion once again. This time it is not simply for the amusement of the bored and wealthy or the healing of the sick and hypochondriac, but for everyone who appreciates the civilised pleasures of a city which is a constantly refreshing delight to the eye and spirit.

Geology, prehistory and the Roman occupation

The history of Bath begins about 150 million years ago, when shallow seas moved across the great mass of the earth that incorporated what was to become Britain. If you look closely at the stone of which the city is built, it is possible to see grains of sand, shells, sometimes tiny fossils, set in the minute egg-shaped particles which are called 'ooliths'. They are a reminder that this soft, pale stone was once part of shifting sediments beneath those remote oceans. Gradually, as lime in the water coated the sand grains, the ground-up fragments of shell and the bones of microscopic animals, they built up to become the massive Jurassic beds of stone that run north and east from Portland in Dorset to the Yorkshire moors. Such stone is called 'freestone', and however it is cut it must be laid within the wall of a building the same way as it lay in the earth. Technically it is known as 'oolitic limestone', and it is quarried from huge blocks separated by vast fissures in the rock. When first cut it is white, but it soon turns to its typical tones of grey, amber and ochre. Even so it remains pale by comparison with many other types of stone, and Jane Austen, accustomed to Hampshire flint and brick, commented on 'the white glare of Bath' when she first visited the city.

The great overflow from the Roman reservoir below the King's Bath

There are still Bath-stone quarries around the city, although many of the old Georgian ones have long since been closed and covered over. At the Camden Works Museum in Bath there is a permanent exhibition on Bath stone, which vividly describes its formation and its subsequent use for building.

It is through the fissures that separate the blocks of Jurassic limestone that the hot springs emerge at a constant temperature of about 49°C (120°F) and a fairly constant flow. The King's Spring, which rises under the steaming green King's Bath below the Pump Room windows, produces well over a quarter of a million gallons a day, and there are two other important springs at the west end of colonnaded Bath Street which have provided more than 24,000 gallons daily both for Roman baths and the old Cross and Hot Baths from medieval times until today.

No-one can know when the hot springs first emerged from the earth, but it was probably more than 100,000 years ago, and the water we

The King's Bath

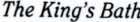

can touch and drink today is likely to have fallen as rain about 10,000 years ago. It seeped down through strata in the stone and was heated deep within the earth, slowly bubbling upwards again into the sunlight.

The medical profession today is generally sceptical about the healing powers of the Bath waters. Hot tap-water, it maintains, is just as beneficial. Nevertheless there are still many believers, and Bath has as good a claim to be a major curative spa as any in Europe. Indeed in the past doctors of every kind – reputable and quack, for that matter – have recommended a course of the Bath waters for various ailments, including rheumatism, arthritis, liver diseases and disorders and a whole host of skin problems from eighteenth-century acne to psoriasis. Scientific analysis has shown the water to contain some thirty different minerals and various trace elements such as calcium, lead, iron, sulphur and magnesium. It is very slightly radioactive and about three times as hard as Bath's normally hard tap-water, since it contains so much dissolved lime. And it is not easy to disprove that some of these factors are not in some way beneficial: a deficiency of zinc, for instance, which is one of the elements in the water, can lead to certain skin diseases. Curiously enough human beings share a predisposition to such diseases with pigs; and legend has it that a herd of pigs first discovered the medicinal qualities of Bath's hot springs for the benefit of mankind.

The pigs were in the charge of a young prince of the west country, Bladud, who had been banished from his father's court because he suffered from leprosy. Condemned to live apart from other men, he earned his bread by tending a herd of pigs. He became aware that they too seemed to be suffering from some skin ailment, until one day when they were rooting in the muddy marshes at the bottom of a remote wooded valley. It was a strange place: although it was winter, there was no frost there, and the mud seemed to be stained blood red where the water oozed from it. Later, Bladud noticed that the black bristled skins of the pigs were healing. He, too, decided to bathe in the muddy waters, and found them curiously warm. It was not long before he realised that he also appeared to be cured. He returned to his father's court, and in time he became king. And he made the place of the hot spring into a sacred place of healing.

It is said that Bladud was the father of Shakespeare's King Lear, and there is probably some old connection between the legend and the stories of the Celtic Iron Age people who settled on the hills around Bath in about 500 BC. They were of that race of whom Julius Caesar said that they measured time not in days, but nights; a warlike, skilled people whose priests were the feared Druids of the sacred

The great head of the Celtic deity Sul

groves, who celebrated such seasonal feasts as Beltane and Lammas. Yet they were not barbarians, and indeed there had been a great deal of trade between Celtic Britain and the Roman Empire before the invasion in AD 43 by the Emperor Claudius – it was evidence of mineral wealth that helped to tempt the Emperor to invade.

The tribe of Iron Age people which held most of the fortified hilltop sites around Bath, like that at Bathampton Down, was the Dobunni. They left no written record, but many artefacts have been excavated by archaeologists over the years, and there is one in particular which gives a vivid clue to the nature of the people the Romans found. It is on display in the Romans Baths Museum, part of the great reconstructed portico of the temple of Sulis-Minerva: the great so-called 'gorgon's head'. Not at all feminine, it is fiercely masculine, with a powerful ferocity and wild glare that is essentially Celtic in form and spirit. It is in sharp contrast to the bland and pretty vacuity of the gilded head of the Roman goddess Minerva, dug up by a workman in 1727 and also on display in the Museum. One senses that the Romans were diplomatically astute in allying this mild-mannered goddess to the unpredictable Celtic Sul, giving him precedence on the temple pediment but enclosing him in Minerva's formal and very Roman embrace of carved Winged Victories and her traditional emblems of dolphin and owl. Certainly it appears that the subjugated inhabitants of the area were reconciled to the linking of Minerva to their own deity of the hot springs.

Within 100 years of the Emperor Claudius's invasion of Britain, Aquae Sulis, as Bath was known to the Romans, was well established. The wealth of Britain may not have come up to expectations and no doubt there were a great many disillusioned Roman legionaries tramping through the sodden wilderness of the countryside, but the hot springs of Aquae Sulis were some comfort. For those descending on the Fosseway into the town, down the old narrow hill called Holloway, which drops down the escarpment of Beechen Cliff on the south side of today's city, the sight of the finely carved buildings, honeyed in the morning sun; the tawny tiled roofs and glint of window glass must have reminded them of home. And it meant civilisation – urban civilisation, on which the whole Empire was based. It meant roads, streets, busy shops and stalls, a theatre, temple, no doubt more than one brothel – and, most important of all, the Roman Baths.

The Roman Baths were first excavated just over 100 years ago, but despite recent exciting finds it is still hard to imagine what the Roman Baths would have been like for those using them over the 400 years of Roman occupation of Britain. Today we see the bones, rather than the flesh, of the great complex of baths that attracted tourists from all parts of the Roman Empire in their time. Such public baths were important social institutions in Roman life: combinations of health farm, pub, golf course, casino and club. The Roman statesman and philosopher, Seneca, described what it sounded like to live rather too close to such an institution:

> *I have lodgings right over a bathing establishment. So picture to yourself the assortment of sounds, which are obnoxious enough to make me hate my very powers of hearing! When your strenuous gentleman, for example, is exercising himself by flourishing leaden weights; when he is working hard, or else pretends to be working hard, I can hear him grunt; and whenever he releases his imprisoned breath, I can hear him panting in wheezy and high-pitched tones. Or perhaps I notice some lazy fellow, content with a cheap rub-down, and hear the crack of the pummelling hand on his shoulder, varying in sound according as the hand is laid on flat or hollow . . .*
>
> *Add to this the arrest of an occasional roisterer or pickpocket, the racket of the man who always likes to hear his own voice in the bathroom, or the enthusiast who plunges into the swimming tank with unconscionable noise and splashing . . . Then the cake-seller with his varied cries, the sausage-man, the confectioner, and all the vendors of food hawking their wares, each with his own distinctive intonation . . .*

It needs some imagination to recreate the Roman Baths of today as they were when as noisy and crowded as Seneca describes. The eye is confused by the excavations of different periods and consequently different levels, with the exposed tile pillars of the hypocausts – the spaces for hot-air circulation beneath the floors that constituted the highly efficient central-heating system – fallen masonry and the debris of centuries. Even the Great Bath, central to the original complex of baths and then, as now, one of the wonders of Britain, is not at once easy to define, altered as it is by being open to the sky and surmounted by Victorian impediments of balustrades and statues.

The entire complex of baths would have been roofed in Roman times, and the Great Bath itself was enclosed first by a timber ceiling and later by a massive stone vault with clerestory windows. To reduce the weight of the roof, hollow box sections were used in the construction. Some of these can be seen where they fell when the baths finally crumbled. But underfoot you can tread where the bare and sandalled feet of those distant Romans strolled 2,000 years ago, on

Gilded bronze head of a statue of the Roman goddess Minerva

the worn limestone paving and the heavy lead sheet that lines the Great Bath. Roman lead pipes still sit neatly in carved gulleys in the stone. And it is still possible to look in awe at the great outfall drain where the overflow spills from the reservoir above the hot springs themselves, the water clear and steaming, the stones stained red with iron oxide.

Beyond the Great Bath spreads the intricate pattern of the surrounding baths and rooms, beyond the colonnaded walks with their once-painted walls. There would have been mosaic floors, tessellated pavements, dark blue and tawny red and frescoed walls, carved and painted cornices and columns. The Roman patrons of the baths would have seen little of the hypocausts we see today and probably thought of them even less, as engineers and slaves supplied and stoked the smouldering charcoal to provide the underfloor hot-air heating that circulated around the *pilae*, or tile pillars.

It was undoubtedly one of the finest such bathing institutions in the Empire. Both men and women used the baths, although at different times, and it is possible that in Aquae Sulis a separate suite for women was built. Everyone met and mingled in the entrance hall whose massive columned windows overlooked the sacred spring itself, the steaming waters of Sulis-Minerva whose great temple rose beyond the pool. Many people no doubt took the opportunity to throw some offering into the water before going into the baths, as we might throw a coin into a fountain, perhaps with some less overt prayer to its pagan spirit. Many exquisitely carved little gemstones were found in the outlet drain during the first excavation of the baths, along with such objects as a gold earring, brooches, bracelets, and a curious curse inscribed backwards on a small piece of lead which began 'May he who carried off Vilbia from me become as liquid as the waters . . .' And when the Victorian floor of the King's Bath was taken up during excavations in 1979, thousands more offerings were discovered. There were some 15,000 coins, a silver rattle, an ivory carving, and pewter vessels, among many such small gifts to the goddess. There were also about forty more curses inscribed on lead scrolls, showing that the petty irritations of life like losing a cloak or a girlfriend were just as important then as now.

All the patrons of the bath changed in a comfortable warm room called the *apodyterium*, and thereafter could make use of all the facilities. Over the years these were vastly extended, so that eventually one might choose one of a number of different ways of spending a refreshing afternoon: relax in the gentle heat of the *tepidarium* before a hot steamy hour in the *caldarium* and a cool swim in a plunge bath, take some vigorous exercise in the spacious open exercise court before a cold dip and a warm swim in the Great Bath, or perhaps have a sauna in the intense dry heat of the *laconicum*. Afterwards there would be a chance to stroll under the colonnades, to sit and gossip or do business over honey cakes and wine. Nor were the ordinary routines of massages, special cleansing and physical exercise neglected. The Romans did not have soap, so instead used light oils and unguents, sometimes sand, stripping away the oil and collected grime with a narrow blade called a *strigil*. The curative properties of the waters, too, were not ignored, particularly in later years. People could sit in comfort up to their necks in the thermal hot water, hoping for some ease of pain from the immersion.

There were other, if less grand and luxurious, public bathing establishments in Aquae Sulis, which also appear to have been dedicated to various gods and goddesses. The town was evidently a cheerful mix of the sacred and secular, both weighted towards sybaritic pleasures which might amuse those with time to kill

One of the Roman hypocausts

and comfort those suffering from some real or imagined illness. Many legionaries came to Aquae Sulis to convalesce and enjoy all the facilities of a successful spa, the theatre, shops, hotels, gambling casinos and the attendant prostitutes. Tourists came from all over the Empire, and many old soldiers retired in and around the town. Many, inevitably, died in Aquae Sulis, and a vast collection of inscribed tombstones and commemorative tablets brings surprisingly vividly to life a whole cross-section of them. Some of them illustrate private tragedies, like the one carved to commemorate a little girl called Successa Petronia, who died aged just three years, four months and nine days, or another, Mercatilla, who was only eighteen months old when she died. Not that everyone died young. One town councillor is recorded as living until he was eighty.

Like most Roman provincial towns, Aquae Sulis was governed from afar by the central government in the persons of the military and political governor of Britain and the financial administrator, known as the procurator. But locally it had

Watercolour by R. Cruikshank
(Bath Reference Library)

its own appointed and elected councillors and magistrates, and although it was a famous spa with a thriving tourist industry, it was also the administrative and trading centre for the surrounding area. Over the centuries it became a Romano-British town, in which many middle-class people spoke Latin, and everyone probably used a colloquial dog-Latin as well as his own Celtic dialect. Out in the countryside the Roman influence was less directly felt, although around Bath there grew up a large concentration of villas built in the Roman style and tradition. There are thirty known sites of considerable importance near the town.

Bath stone, of course, was widely quarried and available for building, but there were other local industries, too. Lead was mined in the Mendips, and it is likely that coal was dug in what were centuries later to become the North Somerset coalfields. Bath also had an important pewter manufacturing industry with particular sites at Camerton, on the Fosseway south of the town, and on top of Lansdown to the north. Aquae Sulis was typical of many Roman towns in acting as the hub of local industry, which flourished under the 400 years of occupation.

Not only was the country itself stimulated by peace and prosperity into demanding all the artefacts of a higher standard of living, but there were expanding markets throughout the Empire for exports. And there was the central Imperial coinage: the Romans fixed a monetary value for every commodity, and thus established a stable economy within which people could rely on trade.

By the beginning of the fourth century AD Aquae Sulis, like most parts of Britain, was enjoying what seemed like a settled and prosperous civilisation. Yet it was to be only a few decades before the first cracks began to show in its walls. Two things began to happen. The Roman Empire itself was starting to crumble. The Barbarians, in the form of such foreign raiders as the Scots, Picts, Franks and Saxons, began to threaten all its borders, and troops were withdrawn from Britain to support other frontiers. In AD 367 it is known that several outlying villas in the Bath area were attacked and set on fire, among them those at Box, Keynsham and Brislington near Bristol, although precisely by whom is not certain. Local anarchy was joining the threat from outside. At the same time the

sea, too, was menacing the stability of Aquae Sulis. It had been almost imperceptibly rising for a century or so, and that meant that the inland water table had also been rising, increasing the danger of flooding. Analysis has been made of the mud deposits found in the hypocausts of the Roman Baths, and it is evident from this that the River Avon began to flood quite regularly, backing up along the drains and outfalls.

At first, the Roman engineers repaired the baths and parts of the temple, both of which were in a slight hollow in the valley. It probably meant that the baths had to be closed for a time to allow repairs to be completed. But by AD 410 the last of the regular Roman army had left Britain. There was no longer any central Roman administration. There were Saxon invasions that could not be contained. And one day there was no-one left to repair the damage to the old bathing establishment, and no point, perhaps, in doing so. The old society had changed. Grass was growing in the streets. The Julian Law, buttress of the Empire, which had forbidden civilians to carry arms, was no longer enforced or upheld, and after 400 years of consistent peace men were once again afraid to move freely in their country.

Aquae Sulis began to crumble. The black silt covered the tessellated pavements and the baths. Columns cracked, roofs fell. As centuries passed it must have made a strange and ghostly ruin, the pale stone, the vaporous marsh, the red-staining waters bubbling out of the reeds. Yet so magnificent were the buildings, even in their decay, that an Anglo-Saxon poet wrote of them:

Wondrous is this masonry, shattered by the Fates. The fortifications have given way, the buildings raised by giants are crumbling. The roofs have collapsed; the towers are in ruins ... There is rime on the mortar. The walls are rent and broken away, and have fallen undermined by age ... Red of hue and hoary with lichen this wall has outlasted kingdom after kingdom, standing unmoved by storms. The lofty arch had fallen. There were splendid palaces and many halls with water flowing through them; a wealth of gables towered aloft ... And so these courts lie desolate, and the framework of the dome with its red arches sheds its tiles ... There stood courts of stone, and a stream gushed forth in rippling floods of hot water ...

In some ways we can feel closer to Roman society than to the Anglo-British society in the centuries that followed. One small fact can bring it home: the Romans used glass for their windows, allowing the sun to warm them. But when they had gone, no-one knew or remembered how to make it any more. It was the beginning of the Dark Ages.

Nineteenth-century commemorative plaque to mark the revelation of the Roman Baths beneath the Pump Room

The end of the Roman Empire. Saxons, Christianity, Medieval Bath

A dark anarchy took hold of Britain after the Romans had been forced to abandon it. The gradual breakdown of the economy, of law and order, communications and trade, reversed the old urban system and made people turn back to their old way of life dependent on the countryside and their own resources. In the south east the Saxons were beginning to colonise the country, but it was a slow and often bloody process. The first real reference to Bath in Saxon documents comes from the Anglo-Saxon Chronicle, written in the ninth century, which mentions the capture of the town in 577. A hundred years later it was established in Saxon territory.

There is very little left of any evidence of the Saxon rule in Bath, except in many of the placenames of the area. A few names remind us of the Celtic British, like Avon, but most of them come from Saxon or Old English. Lansdown, the steep northern hill, means 'long hill', Combe Down, 'hill of the valley', Widcombe, 'wide valley'. Charlecombe, north-east of the city, originally referred to a valley where 'churls', or free peasants, lived. The parish of Walcot in the city itself derives from the small community of native British known as 'wealas', or foreigners, who lived in what is still a pleasantly raffish part of Bath and was then just outside the city wall.

Most impressive of the reminders of the Saxon occupation is the small church tucked away near the river in the old weavers' town of Bradford-on-Avon, a few miles east of Bath. It was quite miraculously preserved, first by becoming a charnel house, and subsequently by being almost lost in vegetation and surrounding buildings, and is now a beautiful and still sacred building. It also gives us some clue as to the beauty and magnificence of the great monastery church established by the Saxons in Bath, belonging to the monastery of St Peter, where in AD 973 the first king of all England was triumphantly crowned.

The coronation of King Edgar on Whit Sunday in that year was a true celebration of a united country. Although he was only thirty when he was crowned, the king had already reigned for some fourteen years in comparative peace, and was to do so for a few years more. There was a glittering procession, tented encampments on the river meadows, and great feasting. For centuries the coronation was commemorated each year with a day's celebration in the town, and although that ceremony finally died out the title 'King of Bath' continued, and was duly awarded to Richard 'Beau' Nash when he became Master of Ceremonies in the early eighteenth century. And it is worth noting that the coronation of all the kings and queens of England has followed the pattern first designed for the crowning of King Edgar at Bath.

Yet less than 100 years later, the Normans invaded England and destroyed almost all the fabric of every Saxon church in the country. The great abbey at Bath was burned in the cause of a local power struggle by Robert de Mowbray. The new king, William II (William Rufus, son of William the Conqueror), conferred the bishopric of Wells on the Norman, John de Villula, and made him a grant of the abbey into the bargain. A physician by profession, Bishop John took a great interest in the hot-spring baths.

Bishop John's great new church was intended to be so vast that the present Abbey occupies only the site of its nave, but it was never finished, although the priory prospered and took over increasing areas of land. The still, dark lakes in the cleft that drops down to the city from Prior Park provided carp for the monks. At Hinton Charterhouse, about six

Abbey Church House

miles south of Bath on the road to Warminster, a Carthusian friary was built in the twelfth century which has survived well enough to give us some real sense of what such a religious institution must have been like. On a fine evening in the small library, as the level sun shines through the window, turning the room into a silent gold-washed shell, you can touch original plaster and imagine those white-robed monks working at their manuscripts, while the fattening doves murmured in the pigeon loft beyond.

But the monks, not only of St Peter's in Bath and Hinton Priory but throughout the country, were becoming rather too prosperous. There were still some great and charitable men among them, like Bishop Reginald Fitzjocelin who founded the Hospital of St John in Bath in 1180, which continues as a charity today to look after old people; but in successive centuries, as ordinary people suffered poverty, the Black Death and subsequent

Above: *Bath Abbey* (Bath Reference Library)

Below: *The Abbey Church by Vertue* (Bath Reference Library)

hardship, the monks grew fat and dissolute. In 1499 the Bishop of Bath and Wells, Oliver King, found that his cathedral church at Bath was almost derelict. He appointed a new prior, William Birde, and together they built a new abbey church in which to set his bishop's chair, the *cathedra*. Only an arch in the south choir was left of the old Norman building: the rest, though much restored by Sir Gilbert Scott in the nineteenth century, is as we know it today.

Bath Abbey is a late example of the English Perpendicular style, and Sir Gilbert Scott's pinnacles, flying buttresses and fine fan vaulting of the roof, although impressive in themselves, might be said to have sadly gilded the original. Nevertheless to the left of the west door you can still look up to the carved stone ladder with its angels and olive tree which is said to commemorate the dream which inspired Bishop Oliver to build his new church.

By the fifteenth century Bath had developed into a small market town well known for its cloth-making industry, although it was by then already beginning to decline. Chaucer's Wife of Bath, Dame Alison, was famous for her skill in the cloth industry, and probably her prototype lived in the weaving village of Twerton 'bisyde Bathe'. Fulling mills, which beat the woven cloth into a kind of solid serge, clacked away below massive weirs along the river. Fuller's earth was dug out of surrounding hills – and indeed was still dug at Odd Down until very recently. And the sheep which yielded the wool grazed lands all round the town. Fairs and markets flourished. Bath's first charter, marking the establishment of a local town council, was granted by Richard I on 7 November 1189. It was the first of many, each one strengthening the power of the corporation while it lessened that of the clergy. When Henry VIII dissolved the monasteries, including St Peter's at Bath, in the sixteenth century, the town council had already taken over a good deal of authority.

In 1574, during a sultry August, Queen Elizabeth I visited Bath and was reported as being decidedly critical of its sewerage arrangements. Cheap Street – cheap meaning market – was the main street, but it was only seven feet wide with an open sewer down the middle. Nor were the baths particularly inviting. The antiquarian John Leland described them as 'much frequentid of people with Lepre, Pokkes, Scabbes and great Aches ... the colour of the water is as it were a depe blewe sea water, and reeketh like a seething Pot continually, having sumwhat a sulphurous and sumwhat an onpleasant savour'. A good deal of cleaning-up was subsequently carried out, and in 1590 the Queen granted the city a new charter which made the corporation the sole power: the church no longer owned even the Abbey churchyard.

Under secular management the hot baths became increasingly popular with visitors, including Anne of Denmark, Queen of James I, who came to find a cure for dropsy in 1616. After the Civil War, when Bath escaped relatively unscathed save for an indecisive battle fought on Lansdown in 1643 between Royalist and Parliamentarian forces, the corporation continued to civilise the city with byelaws containing such injunctions as 'no person shall thrust, cast, or throw another into any of the said Baths with his or her clothes on, under a penalty of six shillings and eightpence'.

In 1668 Samuel Pepys visited the city and although he remarked that 'it cannot be clean to go so many bodies together in the same water', he was agreeably surprised by his dip. Celia Fiennes, one of several resolute lady travellers of the time, sampled the waters, and said 'it tastes like the water that boils eggs'. Much later, Dicken's Sam Weller said it was more like warm flat irons. Excellent descriptions, both.

A pleasant enough place for a visit, Bath, then: the hot baths were an amusing and probably healthy experience, the town was clean enough (there were even public lavatories, known as 'houses of ease') and it was not too far from London. The population was around 3,000, with a summer influx of visitors. So it might have remained. But Bath was just about to be transformed.

Left: *Alleyway from the Abbey Church Yard to Abbey Green.* Below: *The only remaining part of the medieval city wall*

Georgian Bath

At the beginning of the eighteenth century, England was beginning a period of confident expansion which has perhaps never been repeated. There was still poverty, but there was a growing middle class and more widespread prosperity. It was a time when almost anyone might achieve success – and considerable wealth. Some men made money by employing the skill of hand and brain: a young architect called John Wood was among them, although for him money was less important than his vision of a perfect city. Others possessed that entrepreneurial flair which consists of seeing the potential in something everyone else has overlooked, and such a man was Ralph Allen, who came to Bath as a humble assistant to the postmistress and became both rich and famous. And then there were those who were just born lucky: and one of those was an impoverished young Welshman called Richard Nash, who came to Bath early in the eighteenth century and made a small fortune at cards.

Gambling, particularly with cards, was a passion of the time. Faro, Basset, Hazard – these were just three of a score of games of chance in which those with the time and the money (often, indeed, without the money) indulged throughout the winter in London's teeming gaming houses. But in summer London was out of fashion, with most of the aristocracy retiring to their country houses. For many of them the country was even duller than the capital; so where could one go? Oliver Goldsmith observed: 'They wanted some place where they might have each other's company and win each other's money, as they had done during the winter in town.'

And Bath was one of the places where they could do precisely that. It was already becoming more popular when Queen Anne visited it in 1702, and again a year later. Her visit made it fashionable. Daniel Defoe wrote rather sourly: 'We may say now it is the resort of the sound as well as the sick and a place that helps the indolent and the gay to commit that worst of murders – to kill time.'

Not that Bath was yet much more special than other spas like Tunbridge Wells. It was still small, not much bigger than it had been as Aquae Sulis. The Abbey, plainer and stumpier then without Sir Gilbert Scott's Victorian embellishments of flying buttresses and pinnacles, rose from a close and crowded little city, surrounded by open meadows and orchards within the curve of the River Avon. At the East Gate there was a bustling fishmarket on the river quay, and you can still look down at part of the gateway remaining below the north wall of the Empire Hotel – which gives a clue to just how low-lying the whole city then was, particularly along the river. Not that it was a unattractive city: many of its buildings were comparatively new and impressive, although Jacobean in style, with gables and leaded windows. Sally Lunn's House, between Abbey

Below: The Hot Baths in the eighteenth century (Bath Reference Library)

Right: Sally Lunn's house, thought to be the oldest in the city

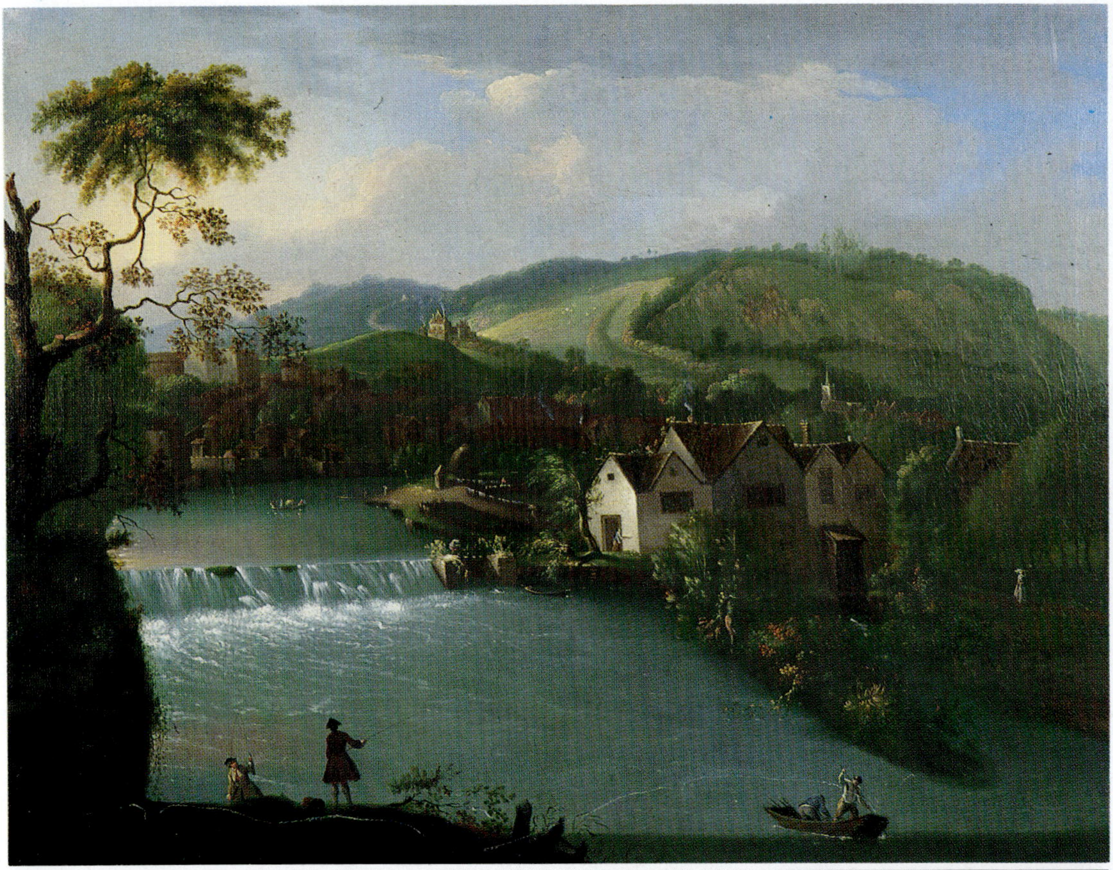

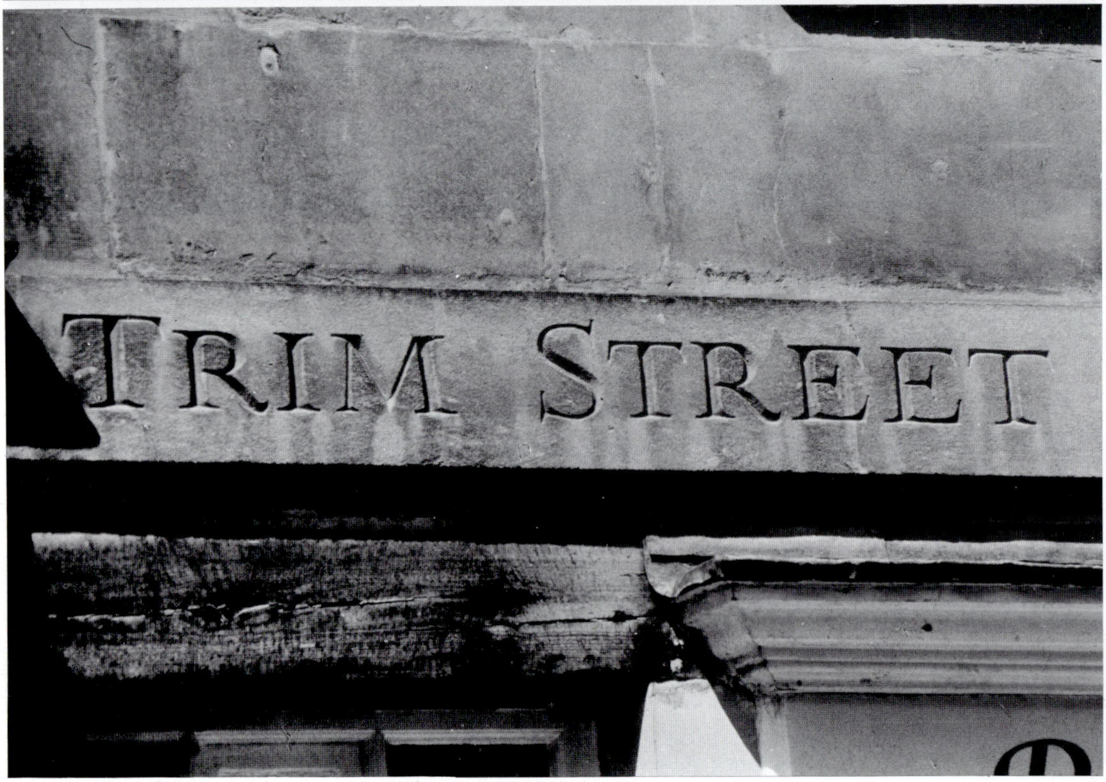
TRIM STREET

Green and the Parade, is typical of them. The Jacobean façade of the house is much more recent than the medieval building behind it, said to be the oldest house in the city.

But there was nothing very pleasant about the kind of society attracted to the city. Visitors to the hot baths brought with them quack doctors, resentful servants and various hangers-on, and encouraged the worst aspects of the inhabitants. The sedan-chair men, vital to the rituals of the Baths since it was they who carried the customers from their lodgings to the hot waters, were a particularly rapacious and ruthless group. Gamblers, in both private and public gaming houses, had little respect for etiquette when in the grip of their passion, and the accompanying amusements such as local balls and musical evenings, were more likely to provoke hooliganism and general misbehaviour than any civilised pleasure. Indeed, after dark it was a dangerous and unsavoury place to be.

The man who changed Bath society and set the scene for the city's architectural transformation was Richard 'Beau' Nash, who was given the unpaid post of Master of Ceremonies by the Corporation when the previous incumbent was killed in a duel. Nash was then thirty-one: flamboyant in dress, immensely confident in manner, genial and enthusiastic and, by chance, relatively wealthy. Not exactly highly educated, despite a spell at Oxford University, but with a not undeservedly high opinion of himself. And he was essentially practical.

Almost immediately Nash forbade duelling and the wearing of swords in the city; persuaded the Corporation to repair the roads, to pave, clean and light the streets, to license the sedan-chair men and regulate their behaviour. He engaged a good orchestra from London and was responsible not only for the building of a new Pump Room, but a large public room, Harrison's Room, for dances as well as gaming on what is now Parade Gardens. He outlawed private gatherings and strictly controlled public ones, and drew up a rigid list of rules to which everyone – and that included dukes, duchesses and even the Prince of Wales – had to conform. It might not have worked had not the age been one in which people were amused by such things: half the amusement of Bath was in obeying the 'King', who was no doubt unaware that he himself was part of the fun. Besides, it worked. Bath was civilised and 'different' – rather like a large, smart holiday camp.

Oliver Goldsmith described the daily ritual thus more or less established for the rest of the century. A diary that might have been typical of the time was kept by one Sophie Carey, eighteen-years old, elder daughter of a widowed colonel in the Footguards who visited Bath in the early 1730s with her father, Aunt Ursula, sister Fanny, and young brother Tom.

We arrived Tuesday: Papa in a most evil mood because we were near two days from London, leaving St Paul's at four in the morning, with a night at the Pelican near Newbury. The guard on the coach informed me one must say 'the Bath' and not plain 'Bath'. He carried a blunderbuss as there are many highwaymen said to be on the road from Chippenham, Tom v. pleased. Lodgings in Westgate Street: clean, but Aunt Ursula shocked to find notice of cock-fighting and a contest for breaking heads advertised in The Bath Journal *in the parlour. Tom v. pleased.*

They rang the Abbey bells when we reached the Bath and Papa was obliged to pay half-a-crown

Above left: *Eighteenth-century view of Bath by Thomas Ross*
(Victoria Art Gallery, Bath City Council)

Left: *Eighteenth-century carved street name*

Below: *Trim Street arch*

to the men. He did not expect to pay so much for everything. Two guineas for the balls, half a guinea to the bookseller. There are subscriptions to the coffee houses and the walks and the Baths. Aunt Ursula says she will bathe every morning at eight and the sedan-chair men charge most excessively although they only carry her a short way. I have been once but agree with Papa that the water tastes unaccountably horrid, although afterwards the Pump Room is amusing and crowded with people. There are public breakfasts later in the morning, sometimes with music or lectures on Art, and hot chocolate and Sally Lunn cakes with butter which Aunt Ursula swears undo all the good of the Baths. She nibbles instead the new biscuits invented by Dr Oliver – for the liver, so she says.

Each day at the Abbey there is a service before noon. There are some tablets on the walls to speak well of people who have died here, and Papa saw one to the memory of General Fitzjohn and said he was damned if he would pray in a place so crammed with hypocrisy. He rides in the afternoon and visits the coffee house to talk news – there are all the newspapers here, even in the ladies' coffee houses, and booksellers circulate all new volumes. Aunt Ursula reads or listens to the spinet before dinner, which is each day at four, and sometimes we are bidden to lectures or classes to Improve Our Minds, but Tom has been every day so far to watch Amazing Troop of Nine Stallions perform The Egyptian Miracle, and Fanny and I prefer to go shopping with Mrs Mountstewart who knows all the best shops and where to buy the best jellies.

On Tuesdays and Thursdays the balls begin at six, v. prompt, and Mr Nash leads out the most noble lord and lady in the minuet to begin the dancing. It was my Lord Baltimore last night and I swear his coat was lined quite throughout with ermine. You cannot escape the dancing for Mr Nash sees everyone and is quite cross if you do not get up when asked for a Country Dance by the most unrefined person. He is a kind man, I believe, but a little odd, and I swear his linen is not altogether clean. Everything must cease at eleven o'clock because he commands it. Papa says he is a fool yet harmless. Papa will not come to the balls unless Mrs Mountstewart is there too, otherwise Tom says he spends the evening in a gaming hall.

Opposite, top: *An eighteenth-century view of the Abbey churchyard before the building of the late eighteenth-century Pump Room* (Bath Reference Library)

Opposite, centre: *Thomas Baldwin's late eighteenth-century colonnaded Bath Street, leading to the Abbey churchyard* (Bath Reference Library)

Opposite, bottom: *Thomas Baldwin's Pump Room in the early nineteenth century* (Bath Reference Library)

Right: *The Garrick's Head public house behind the Theatre Royal, with its bust of the eighteenth-century actor/manager, David Garrick*

Below: *The Abbey Church, 1836 by Millington* (Bath Reference Library)

Sophie would have been able to watch some of the new building going on then in Bath. Even before John Wood's arrival in the city there were changes, and Westgate Street, in which the Careys had lodgings, has buildings whose columns and gables show this state of transition from the seventeenth-century style to what we know as typically Georgian. Sophie might well have admired Beaufort Square, the work of a Bristol architect called John Strahan, who also designed Kingsmead Square with its almost baroque curves. But already John Wood's work was beginning to eclipse these rivals: St John's Hospital, Chandos Court, Ralph Allen's town house (now sadly tucked away behind York Street) and the long-since-demolished Lindsay's Rooms were completed by 1729, and Queen Square and Gay Street were complete by 1734. John Wood's great vision of a Palladian city was taking shape.

Andrea Palladio was a sixteenth-century Italian architect who found inspiration in Roman architecture, and in 1663 his book of research and drawings was published in England. In turn it became the inspiration of the young John Wood who was engaged by the Duke of Chandos to do some work for him in Bath. Later, Wood wrote:

I began to turn my thoughts towards the improvement of the city by building; and for this purpose I procured a plan of the town, which sent me into Yorkshire, in the summer of the year 1725, where I, at my leisure hours, formed one design for the ground at the north-west corner of the city; and another for the land on the north-east side of the town and river.

The Bath Corporation was less excited, however, when the impatient Mr Wood presented them with a scheme for completely rebuilding the city. He was forced to begin his Grand Design in piecemeal fashion: Queen Square was its first real manifestation, and it required a good deal of preliminary persuasion to get it off the ground at all.

First, John Wood had to take a lease on the land from the cautious surgeon who owned it, one Mr Gay. Then he designed the square and sub-let the sites for individual houses to builders, who could plan the interiors but had to stick to his external design. Within seven years, the square was complete. It should be seen as the forecourt of a palace, the north dominating what was then a formal garden of parterre beds with espaliered limes and a low balustrade. Wood also designed the obelisk in the centre, raised by Beau Nash as a tribute to the Prince of Wales with an inscription by the poet Alexander Pope.

John Wood then turned to what he called his Royal Forum. He built the Parades, those plain, harmonious terraces of pale amber stone against the green backdrop of Bathwick Hill, broad paved walks raised on vaults above the marshy riverbank. Behind them, Pierrepont

Below: *North Parade, 1804*
(Bath Reference Library)

Right: *Thomas Rowlandson's cynical eighteenth-century drawings of the 'Comforts of Bath'* *(Bath Reference Library)*

Overleaf: *The Circus – graceful winter silhouettes of plane trees have replaced the original eighteenth-century cobbles*

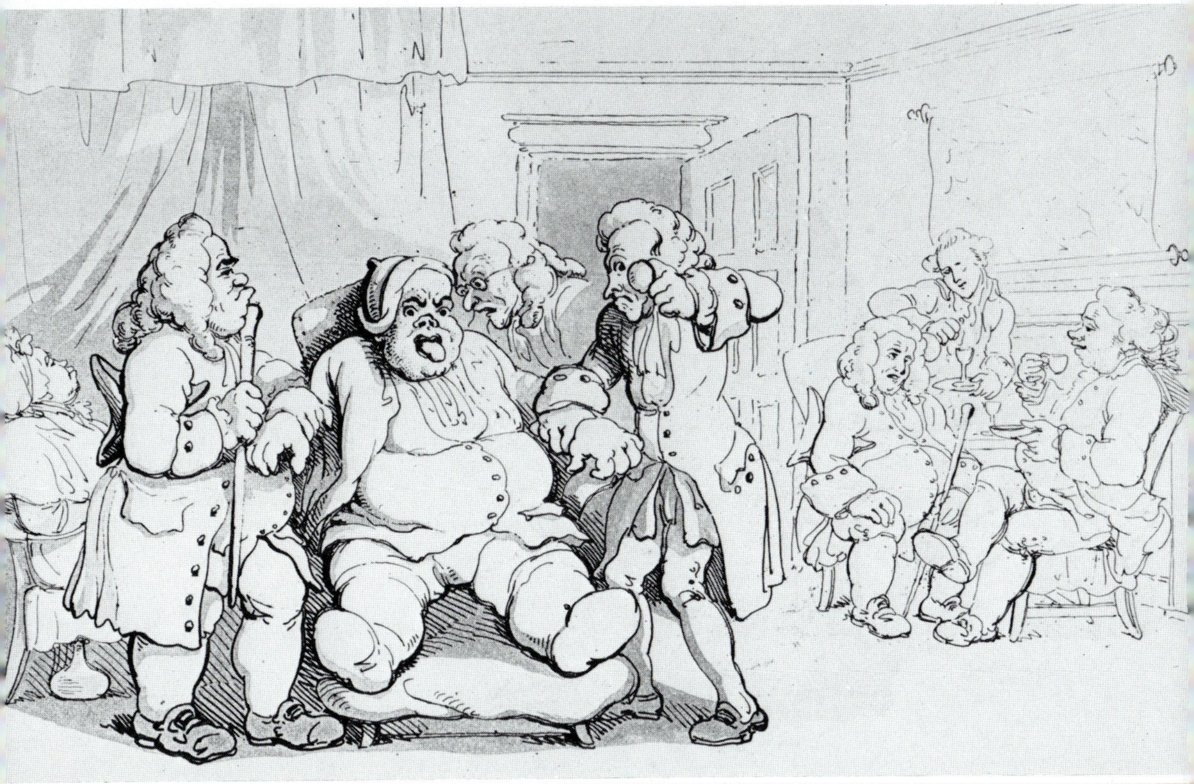

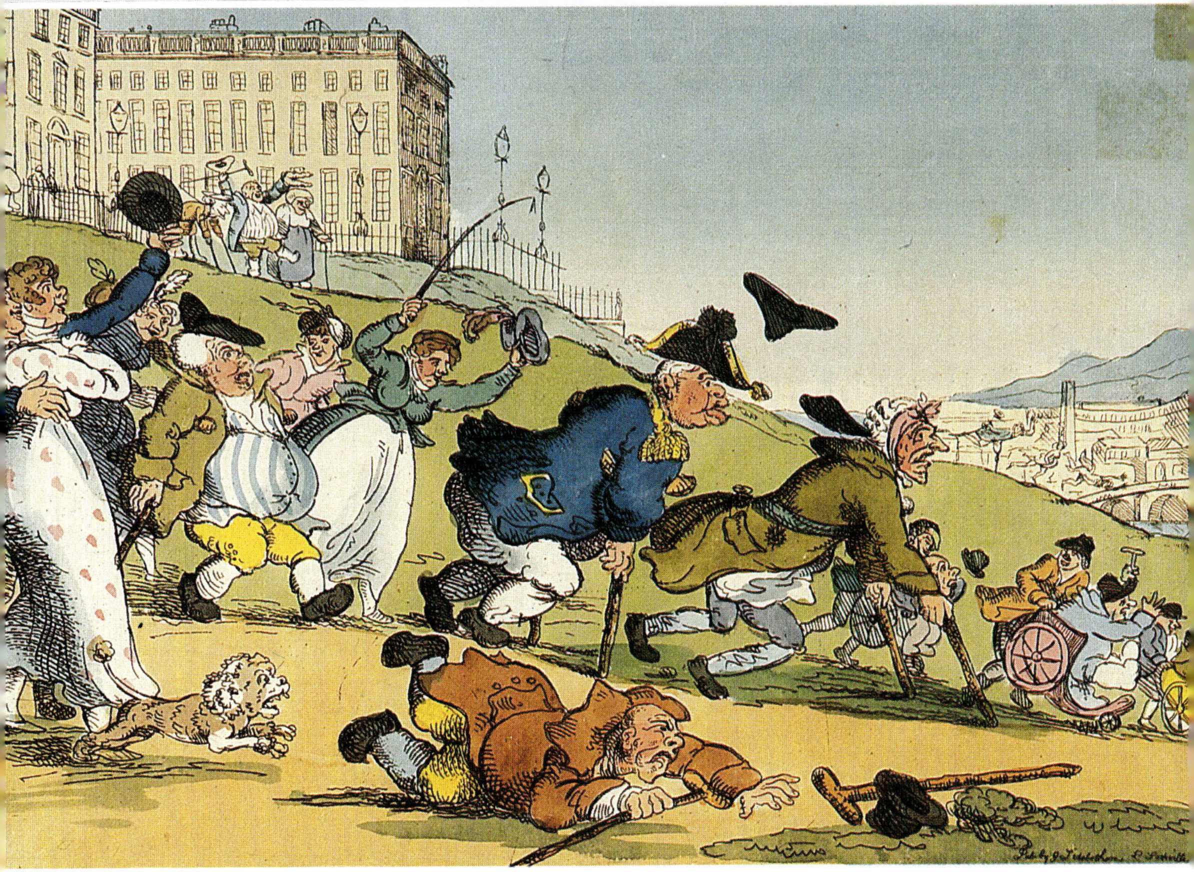

Street. But only in the last year of his life, 1754, did he begin the only great work that fully realises his vision: the Grand Circus. He never lived to see it completed. He was fifty when he died. But his son, John Wood the Younger, was not only to fulfil but crown his father's work, and to begin with he completed this last creation.

The Circus is a Roman amphitheatre translated into domestic architecture. It is composed of three segments, thirty-three houses in all, each varying in size, all built of three storeys, with Roman Doric, Ionic and Corinthian columns. The massive plane trees in the centre, though much loved in the city, are nevertheless not part of the original design: when it was first built the Circus enclosed open cobbles and paving.

John Wood the Younger was as much of a genius as his father. He built Brock Street to link the Circus with what is arguably the most beautiful crescent in Europe, Royal Crescent. Within eight years of the laying of the foundation stone in 1767, the thirty houses that compose this sun-scooping semi-ellipse were complete, curving serenely round a great sloping lawn above the city. No. 1 Royal Crescent is preserved as a perfect example of a Georgian house of the time.

John Wood the Younger died in 1881 at the age of fifty-four, having also completed the Assembly Rooms, which although bombed in 1941, have since been restored by the National Trust. There was little mention made of Wood's passing. By then there were other architects keen to make their name in the city, like Robert Adam, who in 1770 built the elegant and delicate span of Pulteney Bridge, and Thomas Baldwin, the city architect who designed the solemn symmetry of Great Pulteney Street and many other buildings in Bath. There was John Eveleigh, his partner, who designed Grosvenor on the London Road, Somerset Place and Camden Crescent. Both went bankrupt in 1793, and Baldwin's successor, John Palmer, put the final touches to his Pump Room and went on to build the lovely but plainer classical Lansdown Crescent.

Yet the Woods, father and son, remain identified with the spirit as well as the appearance of Bath. High on one of the southern hills, overlooking the city, is the honey-coloured mansion which links the visionary young John Wood with the last of the triumvirate who created Bath as we know it today: the home of Ralph Allen, hard-headed businessman, philanthropist and — literally — man of letters. He arrived in Bath from Cornwall in 1710 to take up a post as assistant to the postmistress.

Ralph Allen's first move was to inform Marshal George Wade, then investigating rumours of Jacobite insurgence in the west country, of the existence of a large cache of arms in the area. Wade was impressed by this shrewd and pleasantly mannered young man, became friendly with him, and later encouraged a match between Allen and his natural daughter. And it was with his backing that Allen de-

Below: *Eighteenth-century view of the Royal Crescent from the Avon by Joseph Farington*
(Victoria Art Gallery, Bath City Council)

Below: *Lansdown Crescent, 1820* (Bath Reference Library)

Above: *Bathwick ferry with a view of Camden Crescent above* (Bath Reference Library)

veloped a system of profitable postal routes, thus earning himself considerable sums from the Post Office. In 1724 he invested in the new Avon Navigation company which was to make the river navigable to Bristol, and two years later began to develop stone quarries on Combe Down.

Bath stone had been neglected for centuries. Allen was determined to exploit it, and he was well aware that Bath was beginning to expand. You can still see the simple houses he built for his quarry workers in Combe Down village, perfect examples of vernacular architecture, and what is now the village recreation ground was once his quarry – the uneven surface gives a clue to the workings beneath. Down what is now called Ralph Allen's Drive he built a railway to carry the blocks of stone, some weighing six tons, down to the river and canal wharf at Widcombe. It was one of the wonders of the day. And nearby he built his great house, Prior Park, designed by John Wood the Elder to display the true beauty and quality of Bath Stone.

Above left: *Pulteney Bridge with Camden Crescent above, from John Wood's Parades* (Bath Reference Library)

Left: *Pulteney Bridge in the eighteenth century* (Bath Reference Library)

Below: *A view of the bridge*

Right: *Early nineteenth-century symmetry in Bath* (Bath Reference Library)

Above: *Combe Down Quarry by Hassell*
(Victoria Art Gallery, Bath City Council)

It was at Prior Park and his town house, also designed by Wood, whom he recognised and encouraged as a young man of original brilliance, that Allen entertained writers, poets, actors and statesmen. The cultured and generous Squire Allworthy in Henry Fielding's novel *Tom Jones* is a portrait of Allen, who had travelled far from his origins as the son of a Cornish innkeeper. But there were many famous names in Bath throughout the eighteenth century: the young Horatio Nelson, recuperating from a fever, not far from the house in which an even younger Emma Hamilton was employed as a servant girl; Dr Johnson visiting his beloved Mrs Thrale, Thomas Gainsborough painting the wealthy at 100 guineas a time; William Herschel playing the organ in the Octagon and discovering the planet Uranus in his spare time, the Duchess of Marlborough complaining about the rule of Beau Nash; almost anyone who was anyone visited Bath to take the waters and gossip in the Pump Room. It was a sparkling century, with aspects both sordid and brutal, but never lacking in vigour, wit and style. Bath was a part of it all. By the beginning of the nineteenth century, when the gaming tables had long been forbidden and the old king buried more than forty years, the city had changed. Tobias Smollet wrote in 1771 that 'a very inconsiderable proportion of genteel people are lost in a mob of impudent plebians', and Christopher Anstey, writer of the scurrilously clever *New Bath Guide*, touched on the kind of people now characterising the place when he described one Simkin Blunderhead, along with Mrs Danglecub and Lady Bumfidget, and their experience in the Baths.

Above: *Prior Park, built by Ralph Allen from Bath stone, which he transported from Combe Down quarry to the river on a steep railway*
(Bath Reference Library)

Nevertheless Bath was still elegant and fashionable, if a trifle less frothy and fizzy – more of a medium sherry than champagne. 'Enchanted castles raised on hanging terraces', observed Smollett's Lydia Melford. Its population had grown to more than 30,000; it had spread far beyond the old walls to incorporate surrounding villages and hills. It was now one of the most beautiful cities in Europe. It was also, it must be said, increasingly impoverished.

The nineteenth century to the present day

The nineteenth century was very different in character from the eighteenth. There was a new mood in the country: a shift from old agricultural wealth to industrial prosperity, a growing sense of the importance of Empire, a zest for technological development – and a new morality. Bath was no longer a crowded cross-section of rich and poor, a scenario for beauty and vulgarity alike, but swiftly turning into a genteel provincial spa to which elderly colonels and unmarried ladies might safely retire, while the small red-light district down by the river – unmentionable in most contemporary guide books – was all that remained of its old improper frivolity. Gradually, the honey-coloured stone was becoming dark with soot as the smoke from Victorian chimneys hung in the valley and Brunel's Great Western Railway linked the city with London and beyond.

Right: *A romantic Victorian view of the city* (Bath Reference Library)

Below: *The Victorian pump room* (Bath Reference Library)

The Kennet and Avon Canal had opened in 1810 to join Bath to London, carrying exports of stone and coal from the North Somerset coalfields, but the venture had been costly and the canal company soon sold out to the railways. Fortunately for us today, the Kennet and Avon Canal still survives, saved by a group of enthusiasts who formed a trust in 1961 to work and campaign for its restoration. Walking along its airy towpath from Widcombe to Bathampton is now one of the pleasantest ways of seeing the city.

Swans languorously skirt the passing canal boats, while today's high-speed trains rumble by along the lower contour of the hill, the city spread below and beyond it. Tiny fretworked iron bridges span the canal, marked with the name Stothert & Pitt, one of several engineering companies begun early in the nineteenth century and still flourishing today.

So Bath adapted to the new industrial age and a newly prosperous middle class. By 1880 businessmen, industrialists, shop-

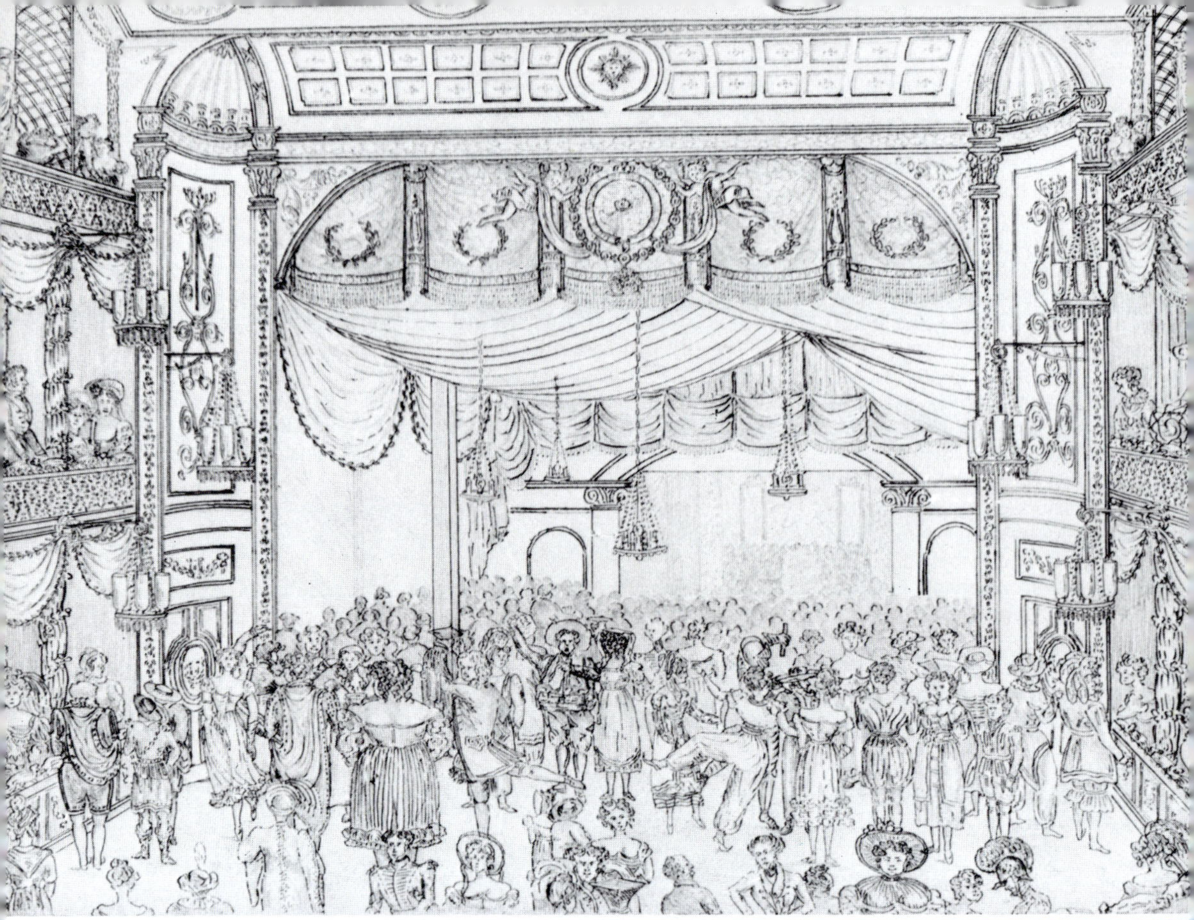

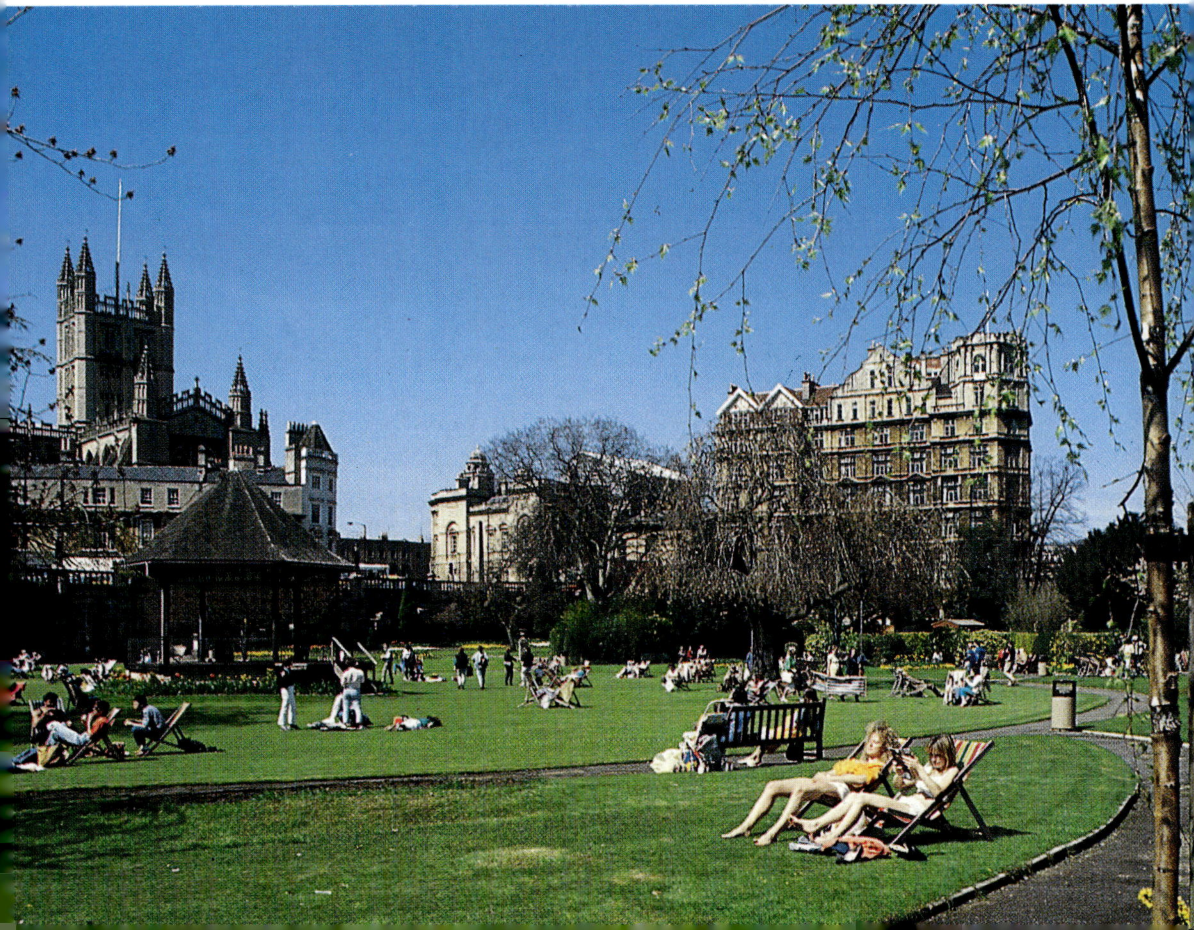

keepers and their families were once more indulging their livers and lumbago in Bath's hot mineral waters, taking it all rather more seriously perhaps than their earlier counterparts. A large number of earnest treatises and medical papers were written on the qualities of Bath water at this time. And to add to the city's attractions, in 1878 the city engineer, Charles Davis, discovered the Roman remains of Aquae Sulis while repairing a leak from the King's Bath.

At the turn of the century Bath was not perhaps as fashionable as in its heyday, but was at least established as a pleasant resort. The Empire Hotel, that Victorian pile opposite the Abbey which was once reviled but now acknowledged as irreplaceable, was a real hotel then instead of offices as it is now. (It is

Above left: *'A Peep At The Fancy', Theatre Royal, 25 April 1824. Drawn by E. Quicke* (Bath Reference Library)

Below left: *Parade Gardens*

Right: *Beechen Cliff, Bath by W. R. Sickert* (Victoria Art Gallery, Bath City Council)

Below: *Bath from Beechen Cliff, with the old southern road into the city in the lower foreground* (Bath Reference Library)

hoped to turn it once more into a hotel in the near future.) Sir Gilbert Scott had embellished the Abbey, there were Roman statues nobly surmounting the Great Bath of Aquae Sulis and bands playing in the newly-laid-out Parade Gardens. Indeed, so much alteration was going on in the city that in 1909 the Bath Preservation Trust was formed, and some years later was responsible for a local Act which ensured that all new building would be either of real Bath Stone or stone with a similiar appearance.

There was to be a great deal more alteration to the city. In 1942 three bombing raids within two nights killed 400 people and destroyed John Wood's Assembly Rooms (although these are now meticulously restored – and the chandeliers had been put prudently in store at the outbreak of the war). Some might say that even more damage was done after the war, when the city planners seemed to have an insatiable desire to demolish all the old Georgian and Victorian artisans' cottages and terraces and replace them with new shopping precincts and blocks of flats – a desire which fortunately did not last quite long enough to destroy everything.

Today Bath is enjoying a new flowering. Only twenty years ago most of its buildings were still stained black by a century or more of smoke, but an intensive campaign to clean up the city has resulted in a restoration of its unparalleled harmony of pale grey and amber stone. It has become fashionable once more, enlivened by its University, founded in 1964, and it is a lure for every kind of shopping indulgence. It remains beautiful at all seasons of the year, as pleasurable an experience as it was 2,000 years ago when a homesick Roman legionary looked down upon its colonnades and porticoes, or 200 years ago when Smollett's young Lydia Melford saw 'enchanted castles'. No-one can leave Bath unrefreshed, or without a sense of gratitude for the gifts of the past.

Marlborough Buildings, 30 Royal Crescent by S. Poole, 1929
(Victoria Art Gallery, Bath City Council)

This page: *The Abbey churchyard*

Front cover, top picture: *North Parade and Duke Street.* **Bottom picture:** *A less than demure view of eighteenth-century Bath – frolics on the lawns below Royal Crescent. Both drawings are by Thomas Rowlandson*
(Bath Reference Library)

Back cover: *The Great Bath, once colonnaded and roofed with vaulted stone*